THIS PLANNER BELONGS TO:

2022 AT A GLANCE

JANUARY 2022

S	M	T	W	T	F	S
						1
2	3	4	5	6	7	8
9	10	11	12	13	14	15
16	17	18	19	20	21	22
23/30	24/31	25	26	27	28	29

FEBRUARY 2022

S	M	T	W	T	F	S
		1	2	3	4	5
6	7	8	9	10	11	12
13	14	15	16	17	18	19
20	21	22	23	24	25	26
27	28					

MARCH 2022

S	M	T	W	T	F	S
		1	2	3	4	5
6	7	8	9	10	11	12
13	14	15	16	17	18	19
20	21	22	23	24	25	26
27	28	29	30	31		

APRIL 2022

S	M	T	W	T	F	S
					1	2
3	4	5	6	7	8	9
10	11	12	13	14	15	16
17	18	19	20	21	22	23
24	25	26	27	28	29	30

MAY 2022

S	M	T	W	T	F	S
1	2	3	4	5	6	7
8	9	10	11	12	13	14
15	16	17	18	19	20	21
22	23	24	25	26	27	28
29	30	31				

JUNE 2022

S	M	T	W	T	F	S
			1	2	3	4
5	6	7	8	9	10	11
12	13	14	15	16	17	18
19	20	21	22	23	24	25
26	27	28	29	30		

JULY 2022

S	M	T	W	T	F	S
					1	2
3	4	5	6	7	8	9
10	11	12	13	14	15	16
17	18	19	20	21	22	23
24/31	25	26	27	28	29	30

AUGUST 2022

S	M	T	W	T	F	S
	1	2	3	4	5	6
7	8	9	10	11	12	13
14	15	16	17	18	19	20
21	22	23	24	25	26	27
28	29	30	31			

SEPTEMBER 2022

S	M	T	W	T	F	S
				1	2	3
4	5	6	7	8	9	10
11	12	13	14	15	16	17
18	19	20	21	22	23	24
25	26	27	28	29	30	

OCTOBER 2022

S	M	T	W	T	F	S
						1
2	3	4	5	6	7	8
9	10	11	12	13	14	15
16	17	18	19	20	21	22
23/30	24/31	25	26	27	28	29

NOVEMBER 2022

S	M	T	W	T	F	S
		1	2	3	4	5
6	7	8	9	10	11	12
13	14	15	16	17	18	19
20	21	22	23	24	25	26
27	28	29	30			

DECEMBER 2022

S	M	T	W	T	F	S
				1	2	3
4	5	6	7	8	9	10
11	12	13	14	15	16	17
18	19	20	21	22	23	24
25	26	27	28	29	30	31

2023 AT A GLANCE

JANUARY 2023

S	M	T	W	T	F	S
1	2	3	4	5	6	7
8	9	10	11	12	13	14
15	16	17	18	19	20	21
22	23	24	25	26	27	28
29	30	31				

FEBRUARY 2023

S	M	T	W	T	F	S
			1	2	3	4
5	6	7	8	9	10	11
12	13	14	15	16	17	18
19	20	21	22	23	24	25
26	27	28				

MARCH 2023

S	M	T	W	T	F	S
			1	2	3	4
5	6	7	8	9	10	11
12	13	14	15	16	17	18
19	20	21	22	23	24	25
26	27	28	29	30	31	

APRIL 2023

S	M	T	W	T	F	S
						1
2	3	4	5	6	7	8
9	10	11	12	13	14	15
16	17	18	19	20	21	22
23/30	24	25	26	27	28	29

MAY 2023

S	M	T	W	T	F	S
	1	2	3	4	5	6
7	8	9	10	11	12	13
14	15	16	17	18	19	20
21	22	23	24	25	26	27
28	29	30	31			

JUNE 2023

S	M	T	W	T	F	S
				1	2	3
4	5	6	7	8	9	10
11	12	13	14	15	16	17
18	19	20	21	22	23	24
25	26	27	28	29	30	

JULY 2023

S	M	T	W	T	F	S
						1
2	3	4	5	6	7	8
9	10	11	12	13	14	15
16	17	18	19	20	21	22
23/30	24/31	25	26	27	28	29

AUGUST 2023

S	M	T	W	T	F	S
		1	2	3	4	5
6	7	8	9	10	11	12
13	14	15	16	17	18	19
20	21	22	23	24	25	26
27	28	29	30	31		

SEPTEMBER 2023

S	M	T	W	T	F	S
					1	2
3	4	5	6	7	8	9
10	11	12	13	14	15	16
17	18	19	20	21	22	23
24	25	26	27	28	29	30

OCTOBER 2023

S	M	T	W	T	F	S
1	2	3	4	5	6	7
8	9	10	11	12	13	14
15	16	17	18	19	20	21
22	23	24	25	26	27	28
29	30	31				

NOVEMBER 2023

S	M	T	W	T	F	S
			1	2	3	4
5	6	7	8	9	10	11
12	13	14	15	16	17	18
19	20	21	22	23	24	25
26	27	28	29	30		

DECEMBER 2023

S	M	T	W	T	F	S
					1	2
3	4	5	6	7	8	9
10	11	12	13	14	15	16
17	18	19	20	21	22	23
24/31	25	26	27	28	29	30

MONTHLY GOALS

NEW GOALS TO FOCUS ON

WHAT WORKED LAST MONTH

WHAT COULD BE BETTER

Beauty is
INSIDE

AUGUST 2022

SUNDAY	MONDAY	TUESDAY	WEDNESDAY	THURSDAY	FRIDAY	SATURDAY
31	1 Summer Bank Holiday (SCT)	2	3	4	5	6
7	8	9	10	11	12	13
14	15	16	17	18	19	20
21	22	23	24	25	26	27
28	29 Summer Bank Holiday (UK except SCT)	30	31	1	2	3

CREATURE OF HABIT

Track new goals or habits and watch your progress every month!

HABIT	1	2	3	4	5	6	7	8	9	10	11	12	13	14	15	16	17	18	19	20	21	22	23	24	25	26	27	28	29	30	31

2022 **AUGUST**

MONDAY
1

DON'T LET WORRYING BLIND
YOU TO THE WONDERFUL!

Summer Bank Holiday (SCT)

TUESDAY
2

WEDNESDAY
3

WHAT DO YOU ***GET*** TO DO,
NOT ***HAVE*** TO DO?

THURSDAY
4

WILDFLOWERS BLOOM IN UNEXPECTED PLACES, AND SO WILL YOU.

FRIDAY
5

SATURDAY
6

BEST. DAY. EVER.

SUNDAY
7

DON'T FORGET:

AUGUST 2022

S	M	T	W	T	F	S
	1	2	3	4	5	6
7	8	9	10	11	12	13
14	15	16	17	18	19	20
21	22	23	24	25	26	27
28	29	30	31			

SEPTEMBER 2022

S	M	T	W	T	F	S
				1	2	3
4	5	6	7	8	9	10
11	12	13	14	15	16	17
18	19	20	21	22	23	24
25	26	27	28	29	30	

THIS WEEK'S HAPPY MOMENT:

2022 **AUGUST**

MONDAY
8

TUESDAY
9

CONSCIOUSLY CREATE THE
LIFE YOU DREAM OF.

WEDNESDAY
10

THURSDAY
11

WRITE DOWN THREE AFFIRMATIONS
AND LET THEM FUEL YOUR DAY!

FRIDAY
12

TRY SOMETHING SURPRISING TODAY.

SATURDAY
13

SUNDAY
14

DON'T FORGET:

AUGUST 2022

S	M	T	W	T	F	S
	1	2	3	4	5	6
7	8	9	10	11	12	13
14	15	16	17	18	19	20
21	22	23	24	25	26	27
28	29	30	31			

SEPTEMBER 2022

S	M	T	W	T	F	S
				1	2	3
4	5	6	7	8	9	10
11	12	13	14	15	16	17
18	19	20	21	22	23	24
25	26	27	28	29	30	

THIS WEEK'S HAPPY MOMENT:

2022 **AUGUST**

MONDAY
15

YOU ARE 100% UNDISTILLED, PURE AMAZING!

TUESDAY
16

WEDNESDAY
17

GIVE YOURSELF THE GRACE AND
PATIENCE YOU EXTEND TO OTHERS.

THURSDAY
18

TAKE TIME TO STRETCH AND
SHOW YOUR BODY SOME TLC!

FRIDAY
19

SATURDAY
20

STAY SOFT—IT'S A
SIGN OF STRENGTH.

SUNDAY
21

DON'T FORGET:

AUGUST 2022

S	M	T	W	T	F	S
	1	2	3	4	5	6
7	8	9	10	11	12	13
14	15	16	17	18	19	20
21	22	23	24	25	26	27
28	29	30	31			

SEPTEMBER 2022

S	M	T	W	T	F	S
				1	2	3
4	5	6	7	8	9	10
11	12	13	14	15	16	17
18	19	20	21	22	23	24
25	26	27	28	29	30	

THIS WEEK'S
HAPPY MOMENT:

2022 **AUGUST**

MONDAY
22

TUESDAY
23

LET YOUR UNIQUE AWESOMENESS
TAKE CENTER STAGE!

WEDNESDAY
24

THURSDAY
25

WHEN WAS THE LAST TIME YOU
WATCHED THE CLOUDS FLOAT BY?

FRIDAY
26

EVEN AFTER EVERYTHING, YOU CAN STILL MAKE SPACE FOR HOPE.

SATURDAY
27

SUNDAY
28

DON'T FORGET:

AUGUST 2022

S	M	T	W	T	F	S
	1	2	3	4	5	6
7	8	9	10	11	12	13
14	15	16	17	18	19	20
21	22	23	24	25	26	27
28	29	30	31			

SEPTEMBER 2022

S	M	T	W	T	F	S
				1	2	3
4	5	6	7	8	9	10
11	12	13	14	15	16	17
18	19	20	21	22	23	24
25	26	27	28	29	30	

THIS WEEK'S HAPPY MOMENT:

MONTHLY GOALS

NEW GOALS TO FOCUS ON

WHAT WORKED LAST MONTH

WHAT COULD BE BETTER

We are ALL a work in PROGRESS

SEPTEMBER 2022

SUNDAY	MONDAY	TUESDAY	WEDNESDAY	THURSDAY	FRIDAY	SATURDAY
28	29	30	31	1	2	3
4 Father's Day (AUS, NZ)	5 Labor Day (USA, CAN)	6	7	8	9	10
11 Patriot Day	12	13	14	15	16	17
18	19	20	21	22	23 Autumn begins (Northern Hemisphere)	24
25 Rosh Hashanah begins	26	27	28	29	30	1

CREATURE OF HABIT

Track new goals or habits and watch your progress every month!

HABIT	1	2	3	4	5	6	7	8	9	10	11	12	13	14	15	16	17	18	19	20	21	22	23	24	25	26	27	28	29	30	31

2022 AUGUST/SEPTEMBER

MONDAY
29

FOCUSED AND FLOURISHING!

Summer Bank Holiday (UK except SCT)

TUESDAY
30

WEDNESDAY
31

DON'T LET THE STRESS OF TODAY
DRAG DOWN YOUR WEEK.

THURSDAY
1

STATUS: TAKING A MENTAL VACATION.

FRIDAY
2

SATURDAY
3

STOP APOLOGIZING.

SUNDAY
4

Father's Day (AUS, NZ)

DON'T FORGET:

SEPTEMBER 2022

S	M	T	W	T	F	S
				1	2	3
4	5	6	7	8	9	10
11	12	13	14	15	16	17
18	19	20	21	22	23	24
25	26	27	28	29	30	

OCTOBER 2022

S	M	T	W	T	F	S
						1
2	3	4	5	6	7	8
9	10	11	12	13	14	15
16	17	18	19	20	21	22
23/30	24/31	25	26	27	28	29

THIS WEEK'S HAPPY MOMENT:

2022 **SEPTEMBER**

MONDAY
5

Labor Day (USA, CAN)

TUESDAY
6

THE WAY YOU SPEAK TO YOURSELF MATTERS.

WEDNESDAY
7

THURSDAY
8

CURIOSITY IS YOUR SUPERPOWER.
WHAT WILL YOU DISCOVER?

FRIDAY
9

BE A FROOT LOOP IN A WORLD OF CHEERIOS.

SATURDAY
10

SUNDAY
11

Patriot Day

DON'T FORGET:

THIS WEEK'S HAPPY MOMENT:

SEPTEMBER 2022

S	M	T	W	T	F	S
				1	2	3
4	5	6	7	8	9	10
11	12	13	14	15	16	17
18	19	20	21	22	23	24
25	26	27	28	29	30	

OCTOBER 2022

S	M	T	W	T	F	S
						1
2	3	4	5	6	7	8
9	10	11	12	13	14	15
16	17	18	19	20	21	22
23/30	24/31	25	26	27	28	29

2022 **SEPTEMBER**

MONDAY
12

DON'T WORRY, EVERYTHING
WILL GET DONE IN ITS TIME.

TUESDAY
13

WEDNESDAY
14

RESET. REFRESH. RELAX.

THURSDAY
15

THIS IS PERMISSION TO "WASTE" TODAY WISELY. HAVE SOME FUN!

FRIDAY 16

SATURDAY 17

SUNDAY 18

GET LOST FOR A WHILE AND YOU JUST MIGHT END UP FINDING YOURSELF.

DON'T FORGET:

SEPTEMBER 2022

S	M	T	W	T	F	S
				1	2	3
4	5	6	7	8	9	10
11	12	13	14	15	16	17
18	19	20	21	22	23	24
25	26	27	28	29	30	

OCTOBER 2022

S	M	T	W	T	F	S
						1
2	3	4	5	6	7	8
9	10	11	12	13	14	15
16	17	18	19	20	21	22
23/30	24/31	25	26	27	28	29

THIS WEEK'S HAPPY MOMENT:

2022 **SEPTEMBER**

MONDAY
19

TUESDAY
20

CHERISH THE SIMPLE THINGS. JOY CAN HIDE IN THE MOST OBVIOUS PLACES!

WEDNESDAY
21

THURSDAY
22

TODAY IS YOUR DAY! CAN YOU FEEL IT?

FRIDAY
23

Autumn begins (Northern Hemisphere)

EASY MATH:
YOU + SMILE =
POWERFUL DUO

SATURDAY
24

SUNDAY
25

Rosh Hashanah begins

DON'T FORGET:

THIS WEEK'S
HAPPY MOMENT:

SEPTEMBER 2022

S	M	T	W	T	F	S
				1	2	3
4	5	6	7	8	9	10
11	12	13	14	15	16	17
18	19	20	21	22	23	24
25	26	27	28	29	30	

OCTOBER 2022

S	M	T	W	T	F	S
						1
2	3	4	5	6	7	8
9	10	11	12	13	14	15
16	17	18	19	20	21	22
23/30	24/31	25	26	27	28	29

2022 **SEPTEMBER/OCTOBER**

MONDAY
26

SKIP THE RUMINATING AND JUST ***BE***.

TUESDAY
27

WEDNESDAY
28

IF NOT NOW, WHEN?

THURSDAY
29

WHAT MADE YOU LAUGH
RECENTLY? BOOKMARK IT!

FRIDAY
30

SATURDAY
1

THERE'S ALWAYS ROOM
FOR MORE ZEN.

SUNDAY
2

DON'T FORGET:

SEPTEMBER 2022

S	M	T	W	T	F	S
				1	2	3
4	5	6	7	8	9	10
11	12	13	14	15	16	17
18	19	20	21	22	23	24
25	26	27	28	29	30	

OCTOBER 2022

S	M	T	W	T	F	S
						1
2	3	4	5	6	7	8
9	10	11	12	13	14	15
16	17	18	19	20	21	22
23/30	24/31	25	26	27	28	29

THIS WEEK'S
HAPPY MOMENT:

MONTHLY GOALS

NEW GOALS TO FOCUS ON

WHAT WORKED LAST MONTH

WHAT COULD BE BETTER

THIS
TOO SHALL
PASS

OCTOBER 2022

SUNDAY	MONDAY	TUESDAY	WEDNESDAY	THURSDAY	FRIDAY	SATURDAY
25	26	27	28	29	30	1
2	3	4 Yom Kippur begins	5	6	7	8
9 Sukkot begins	10 Columbus Day (USA); Indigenous Peoples' Day (USA); Thanksgiving Day (CAN)	11	12	13	14	15
16	17	18	19	20	21	22
23/30	24/31 Diwali begins (24th); Halloween (31st)	25	26	27	28	29

CREATURE OF HABIT

Track new goals or habits and watch your progress every month!

HABIT	1	2	3	4	5	6	7	8	9	10	11	12	13	14	15	16	17	18	19	20	21	22	23	24	25	26	27	28	29	30	31

2022 **OCTOBER**

MONDAY
3

TUESDAY
4

WHAT BROUGHT YOU PEACE THIS WEEK?

Yom Kippur begins

WEDNESDAY
5

THURSDAY
6

YOU ARE THE STAR OF YOUR OWN STORY—AND THE AUTHOR.

FRIDAY
7

THERE IS NO RIGHT
OR WRONG WAY,
JUST YOUR WAY.

SATURDAY
8

SUNDAY
9

Sukkot begins

DON'T FORGET:

OCTOBER 2022

S	M	T	W	T	F	S
						1
2	3	4	5	6	7	8
9	10	11	12	13	14	15
16	17	18	19	20	21	22
23/30	24/31	25	26	27	28	29

NOVEMBER 2022

S	M	T	W	T	F	S
		1	2	3	4	5
6	7	8	9	10	11	12
13	14	15	16	17	18	19
20	21	22	23	24	25	26
27	28	29	30			

THIS WEEK'S
HAPPY MOMENT:

2022 **OCTOBER**

MONDAY
10

YOU CAN AND YOU WILL.

Columbus Day (USA); Indigenous Peoples' Day (USA); Thanksgiving Day (CAN)

TUESDAY
11

WEDNESDAY
12

TIDY UP TODAY. A FRESHLY CLEANED SPACE IS A LUXURY FOR A BUSY MIND!

THURSDAY
13

TAKE A DEEP BREATH. YOU MADE IT. IT'S FRIDAY!

FRIDAY 14

SATURDAY 15

SUNDAY 16

MAKE TIME TO CLEAR THE CACHE.

DON'T FORGET:

OCTOBER 2022

S	M	T	W	T	F	S
						1
2	3	4	5	6	7	8
9	10	11	12	13	14	15
16	17	18	19	20	21	22
23/30	24/31	25	26	27	28	29

NOVEMBER 2022

S	M	T	W	T	F	S
		1	2	3	4	5
6	7	8	9	10	11	12
13	14	15	16	17	18	19
20	21	22	23	24	25	26
27	28	29	30			

THIS WEEK'S HAPPY MOMENT:

2022 OCTOBER

MONDAY
17

TUESDAY
18

NUMBERS CAN'T COUNT HOW BRILLIANTLY COMPLEX YOU ARE!

WEDNESDAY
19

THURSDAY
20

UNLOCK YOUR POTENTIAL.

FRIDAY
21

EVEN IF YOU CAN'T SEE IT, BLUE SKY IS ALWAYS THERE.

SATURDAY
22

SUNDAY
23

DON'T FORGET:

OCTOBER 2022

S	M	T	W	T	F	S
						1
2	3	4	5	6	7	8
9	10	11	12	13	14	15
16	17	18	19	20	21	22
23/30	24/31	25	26	27	28	29

NOVEMBER 2022

S	M	T	W	T	F	S
		1	2	3	4	5
6	7	8	9	10	11	12
13	14	15	16	17	18	19
20	21	22	23	24	25	26
27	28	29	30			

THIS WEEK'S HAPPY MOMENT:

2022 **OCTOBER**

MONDAY 24

THERE IS AN INNER CHILD IN ALL OF US. DO SOMETHING SILLY TODAY!

Diwali begins

TUESDAY 25

WEDNESDAY 26

JUST SAY "YIKES" AND MOVE ON!

THURSDAY 27

YOU ARE SAFE TO BE YOUR
TRUE, AUTHENTIC SELF.

FRIDAY
28

SATURDAY
29

REPEAT: I AM RESILIENT.

SUNDAY
30

DON'T FORGET:

THIS WEEK'S
HAPPY MOMENT:

OCTOBER 2022

S	M	T	W	T	F	S
						1
2	3	4	5	6	7	8
9	10	11	12	13	14	15
16	17	18	19	20	21	22
23/30	24/31	25	26	27	28	29

NOVEMBER 2022

S	M	T	W	T	F	S
		1	2	3	4	5
6	7	8	9	10	11	12
13	14	15	16	17	18	19
20	21	22	23	24	25	26
27	28	29	30			

MONTHLY GOALS

NEW GOALS TO FOCUS ON

WHAT WORKED LAST MONTH

WHAT COULD BE BETTER

BE PATIENT

AND DON'T

GIVE UP!

NOVEMBER 2022

SUNDAY	MONDAY	TUESDAY	WEDNESDAY	THURSDAY	FRIDAY	SATURDAY
30	31	1	2	3	4	5
6 Daylight Saving Time ends (USA, CAN)	7	8 Election Day	9	10	11 Veterans Day (USA); Remembrance Day (CAN, UK)	12
13	14	15	16	17	18	19
20	21	22	23	24 Thanksgiving Day	25	26
27	28	29	30 St. Andrew's Day (SCT)	1	2	3

CREATURE OF HABIT

Track new goals or habits and watch your progress every month!

HABIT	1	2	3	4	5	6	7	8	9	10	11	12	13	14	15	16	17	18	19	20	21	22	23	24	25	26	27	28	29	30	31

2022 OCTOBER/NOVEMBER

MONDAY
31

Halloween

TUESDAY
1

THE BEST REVENGE IS NONE.
MOVE ON, AND MOVE FORWARD.

WEDNESDAY
2

THURSDAY
3

DON'T FORGET TO GO SHARE SOME LOVE.

FRIDAY
4

HAPPINESS IS A FORM OF COURAGE.

SATURDAY
5

SUNDAY
6

Daylight Saving Time ends (USA, CAN)

DON'T FORGET:

NOVEMBER 2022

S	M	T	W	T	F	S
		1	2	3	4	5
6	7	8	9	10	11	12
13	14	15	16	17	18	19
20	21	22	23	24	25	26
27	28	29	30			

DECEMBER 2022

S	M	T	W	T	F	S
				1	2	3
4	5	6	7	8	9	10
11	12	13	14	15	16	17
18	19	20	21	22	23	24
25	26	27	28	29	30	31

THIS WEEK'S HAPPY MOMENT:

2022 NOVEMBER

MONDAY
7

GO MAKE SOMEONE'S DAY!
HOW'D IT FEEL?

TUESDAY
8

Election Day

WEDNESDAY
9

GO TO BED EARLY TONIGHT. YOUR BODY
WILL THANK YOU IN THE MORNING!

THURSDAY
10

THERE'S SO MUCH TO LOOK FORWARD TO.

FRIDAY 11

Veterans Day (USA); Remembrance Day (CAN, UK)

SATURDAY 12

TODAY'S MANTRA: C'EST LA VIE!

SUNDAY 13

DON'T FORGET:

NOVEMBER 2022

S	M	T	W	T	F	S
		1	2	3	4	5
6	7	8	9	10	11	12
13	14	15	16	17	18	19
20	21	22	23	24	25	26
27	28	29	30			

DECEMBER 2022

S	M	T	W	T	F	S
				1	2	3
4	5	6	7	8	9	10
11	12	13	14	15	16	17
18	19	20	21	22	23	24
25	26	27	28	29	30	31

THIS WEEK'S HAPPY MOMENT:

2022 NOVEMBER

MONDAY
14

TUESDAY
15

CATCH UP WITH AN OLD FRIEND. IT COULD BE THE FRESH START YOU NEED!

WEDNESDAY
16

THURSDAY
17

GROUND YOURSELF IN GRATITUDE.

FRIDAY
18

USING YOUR VOICE IS THE MOST POWERFUL TOOL YOU HAVE.

SATURDAY
19

SUNDAY
20

DON'T FORGET:

NOVEMBER 2022

S	M	T	W	T	F	S
		1	2	3	4	5
6	7	8	9	10	11	12
13	14	15	16	17	18	19
20	21	22	23	24	25	26
27	28	29	30			

DECEMBER 2022

S	M	T	W	T	F	S
				1	2	3
4	5	6	7	8	9	10
11	12	13	14	15	16	17
18	19	20	21	22	23	24
25	26	27	28	29	30	31

THIS WEEK'S HAPPY MOMENT:

2022 **NOVEMBER**

MONDAY
21

BE GENEROUS IN YOUR
SPIRIT, HEART, AND TIME.

TUESDAY
22

WEDNESDAY
23

THERE'S NOTHING BETTER THAN
BEING ***FULL*** OF LOVE!

THURSDAY
24

Thanksgiving Day

WHEN WAS THE LAST TIME YOU TOOK A NAP? TREAT YOURSELF TODAY!

FRIDAY 25

SATURDAY 26

JUST KEEP DOING WHAT YOU CAN.

SUNDAY 27

DON'T FORGET:

NOVEMBER 2022

S	M	T	W	T	F	S
		1	2	3	4	5
6	7	8	9	10	11	12
13	14	15	16	17	18	19
20	21	22	23	24	25	26
27	28	29	30			

DECEMBER 2022

S	M	T	W	T	F	S
				1	2	3
4	5	6	7	8	9	10
11	12	13	14	15	16	17
18	19	20	21	22	23	24
25	26	27	28	29	30	31

THIS WEEK'S HAPPY MOMENT:

MONTHLY GOALS

NEW GOALS TO FOCUS ON

WHAT WORKED LAST MONTH

WHAT COULD BE BETTER

MAKE
Mistakes
YOU'RE
HUMAN
NOT A
Robot

DECEMBER 2022

SUNDAY	MONDAY	TUESDAY	WEDNESDAY	THURSDAY	FRIDAY	SATURDAY
27	28	29	30	1	2	3
4	5	6	7 Pearl Harbor Day	8	9	10
11	12	13	14	15	16	17
18 Hanukkah begins	19	20	21 Winter begins (Northern Hemisphere)	22	23	24 Christmas Eve
25 Christmas Day	26 Kwanzaa begins; Boxing Day (AUS, CAN, NZ, UK)	27	28	29	30	31 New Year's Eve

CREATURE OF HABIT

Track new goals or habits and watch your progress every month!

HABIT	1	2	3	4	5	6	7	8	9	10	11	12	13	14	15	16	17	18	19	20	21	22	23	24	25	26	27	28	29	30	31

2022 NOVEMBER/DECEMBER

MONDAY
28

TUESDAY
29

BE SOMEBODY WHO MAKES
EVERYBODY FEEL LIKE SOMEBODY.

WEDNESDAY
30

St. Andrew's Day (SCT)

THURSDAY
1

TREAT YOURSELF TO A SECOND HELPING OF KINDNESS.

FRIDAY
2

SPARKLE ALL THE WAY.

SATURDAY
3

SUNDAY
4

DON'T FORGET:

THIS WEEK'S HAPPY MOMENT:

DECEMBER 2022

S	M	T	W	T	F	S
				1	2	3
4	5	6	7	8	9	10
11	12	13	14	15	16	17
18	19	20	21	22	23	24
25	26	27	28	29	30	31

JANUARY 2023

S	M	T	W	T	F	S
1	2	3	4	5	6	7
8	9	10	11	12	13	14
15	16	17	18	19	20	21
22	23	24	25	26	27	28
29	30	31				

2022 DECEMBER

MONDAY
5

FEELING STRESSED? WHY NOT TAKE A ME DAY? OR A ME WEEK?

TUESDAY
6

WEDNESDAY
7

LET YOUR SOUL SHINE.

Pearl Harbor Day

THURSDAY
8

GIVE A STRANGER A COMPLIMENT.
YOU'LL BOTH FEEL GREAT!

FRIDAY
9

SATURDAY
10

YOU'RE NOT WEIRD.
YOU'RE LIMITED EDITION!

SUNDAY
11

DON'T FORGET:

DECEMBER 2022

S	M	T	W	T	F	S
				1	2	3
4	5	6	7	8	9	10
11	12	13	14	15	16	17
18	19	20	21	22	23	24
25	26	27	28	29	30	31

JANUARY 2023

S	M	T	W	T	F	S
1	2	3	4	5	6	7
8	9	10	11	12	13	14
15	16	17	18	19	20	21
22	23	24	25	26	27	28
29	30	31				

THIS WEEK'S
HAPPY MOMENT:

2022 **DECEMBER**

MONDAY
12

TUESDAY
13

BE MERRY AND BRIGHT!

WEDNESDAY
14

THURSDAY
15

SPICE UP YOUR LIFE BY TRYING SOMETHING NEW. IT MAY SURPRISE YOU!

FRIDAY
16

THERE IS NO SHAME IN A SLOW CLIMB.

SATURDAY
17

SUNDAY
18

Hanukkah begins

DON'T FORGET:

DECEMBER 2022

S	M	T	W	T	F	S
				1	2	3
4	5	6	7	8	9	10
11	12	13	14	15	16	17
18	19	20	21	22	23	24
25	26	27	28	29	30	31

JANUARY 2023

S	M	T	W	T	F	S
1	2	3	4	5	6	7
8	9	10	11	12	13	14
15	16	17	18	19	20	21
22	23	24	25	26	27	28
29	30	31				

THIS WEEK'S HAPPY MOMENT:

2022 DECEMBER

MONDAY
19

'TIS THE SEASON TO BE JOYFUL!

TUESDAY
20

WEDNESDAY
21

THERE IS NO RIGHT WAY TO FEEL RIGHT NOW.

Winter begins (Northern Hemisphere)

THURSDAY
22

FRIDAY
30

THIS IS THE TIME TO
MOVE FORWARD.
YOU CAN DO IT!

SATURDAY
31

New Year's Eve

SUNDAY
1

New Year's Day

DON'T FORGET:

DECEMBER 2022

S	M	T	W	T	F	S
				1	2	3
4	5	6	7	8	9	10
11	12	13	14	15	16	17
18	19	20	21	22	23	24
25	26	27	28	29	30	31

JANUARY 2023

S	M	T	W	T	F	S
1	2	3	4	5	6	7
8	9	10	11	12	13	14
15	16	17	18	19	20	21
22	23	24	25	26	27	28
29	30	31				

THIS WEEK'S
HAPPY MOMENT:

MONTHLY GOALS

NEW GOALS TO FOCUS ON

WHAT WORKED LAST MONTH

WHAT COULD BE BETTER

Attitude
IS A LITTLE THING
that makes
A BIG DIFFERENCE

JANUARY 2023

SUNDAY	MONDAY	TUESDAY	WEDNESDAY	THURSDAY	FRIDAY	SATURDAY
1 New Year's Day	2 Day after New Year's Day (NZ, SCT)	3	4	5	6	7
8	9	10	11	12	13	14
15	16 Martin Luther King Jr. Day	17	18	19	20	21
22 Chinese New Year	23	24	25	26 Australia Day (AUS)	27	28
29	30	31	1	2	3	4

CREATURE OF HABIT

Track new goals or habits and watch your progress every month!

HABIT	1	2	3	4	5	6	7	8	9	10	11	12	13	14	15	16	17	18	19	20	21	22	23	24	25	26	27	28	29	30	31

2023 **JANUARY**

MONDAY
2

THIS YEAR IS FOR BLOOMING.

Day after New Year's Day (NZ, SCT)

TUESDAY
3

WEDNESDAY
4

YOU ARE 100% WORTH IT.

THURSDAY
5

RESOLUTION #1: MORE JOY,
MORE WONDER, MORE YOU!

FRIDAY
6

SATURDAY
7

RADIATE POSITIVITY!

SUNDAY
8

DON'T FORGET:

THIS WEEK'S
HAPPY MOMENT:

JANUARY 2023

S	M	T	W	T	F	S
1	2	3	4	5	6	7
8	9	10	11	12	13	14
15	16	17	18	19	20	21
22	23	24	25	26	27	28
29	30	31				

FEBRUARY 2023

S	M	T	W	T	F	S
			1	2	3	4
5	6	7	8	9	10	11
12	13	14	15	16	17	18
19	20	21	22	23	24	25
26	27	28				

2023 **JANUARY**

MONDAY
9

TUESDAY
10

FIND A WAY TO PAY IT FORWARD TODAY!

WEDNESDAY
11

THURSDAY
12

YOU CAN'T STOP CHANGE FROM HAPPENING, SO HOW WILL YOU EVOLVE?

FRIDAY
13

ALWAYS FEEL
FREE TO JUST BE.

SATURDAY
14

SUNDAY
15

DON'T FORGET:

JANUARY 2023

S	M	T	W	T	F	S
1	2	3	4	5	6	7
8	9	10	11	12	13	14
15	16	17	18	19	20	21
22	23	24	25	26	27	28
29	30	31				

FEBRUARY 2023

S	M	T	W	T	F	S
			1	2	3	4
5	6	7	8	9	10	11
12	13	14	15	16	17	18
19	20	21	22	23	24	25
26	27	28				

THIS WEEK'S
HAPPY MOMENT:

MONDAY
16

BE KIND WITH A SPINE.

Martin Luther King Jr. Day

TUESDAY
17

WEDNESDAY
18

YOU ARE IN CHARGE OF BUILDING YOURSELF UP, NOT TEARING YOURSELF DOWN.

THURSDAY
19

INHALE. EXHALE. YOU'VE GOT THIS.

FRIDAY 20

SATURDAY 21

SUNDAY 22

BE IN THE BUSINESS OF BLISS.

Chinese New Year

DON'T FORGET:

THIS WEEK'S HAPPY MOMENT:

JANUARY 2023

S	M	T	W	T	F	S
1	2	3	4	5	6	7
8	9	10	11	12	13	14
15	16	17	18	19	20	21
22	23	24	25	26	27	28
29	30	31				

FEBRUARY 2023

S	M	T	W	T	F	S
			1	2	3	4
5	6	7	8	9	10	11
12	13	14	15	16	17	18
19	20	21	22	23	24	25
26	27	28				

MONDAY
23

TUESDAY
24

DO NOT EXPECT PERFECTION IN EVERY SITUATION. WE ARE ONLY HUMAN, AFTER ALL!

WEDNESDAY
25

THURSDAY
26

ACT WITH LOVE FIRST. REMEMBER THAT OTHERS MAY BE FACING STRUGGLES TOO.

Australia Day (AUS)

FRIDAY
27

TIME TO RISE
AND CONQUER!

SATURDAY
28

SUNDAY
29

DON'T FORGET:

JANUARY 2023

S	M	T	W	T	F	S
1	2	3	4	5	6	7
8	9	10	11	12	13	14
15	16	17	18	19	20	21
22	23	24	25	26	27	28
29	30	31				

FEBRUARY 2023

S	M	T	W	T	F	S
			1	2	3	4
5	6	7	8	9	10	11
12	13	14	15	16	17	18
19	20	21	22	23	24	25
26	27	28				

THIS WEEK'S
HAPPY MOMENT:

MONTHLY GOALS

NEW GOALS TO FOCUS ON

WHAT WORKED LAST MONTH

WHAT COULD BE BETTER

YOU ARE
Cute
AND YOU
DESERVE A
Break

FEBRUARY 2023

SUNDAY	MONDAY	TUESDAY	WEDNESDAY	THURSDAY	FRIDAY	SATURDAY
29	30	31	1	2 Groundhog Day	3	4
5	6 Waitangi Day (NZ)	7	8	9	10	11
12 Abraham Lincoln's Birthday	13	14 Valentine's Day	15	16	17	18
19	20 Presidents' Day	21	22 Ash Wednesday (Lent begins)	23	24	25
26	27	28	1	2	3	4

CREATURE OF HABIT

Track new goals or habits and watch your progress every month!

HABIT	1	2	3	4	5	6	7	8	9	10	11	12	13	14	15	16	17	18	19	20	21	22	23	24	25	26	27	28	29	30	31

2023 JANUARY/FEBRUARY

MONDAY
30

POSITIVE VIBES + MAXIMUM EFFORT = NO LIMITS!

TUESDAY
31

WEDNESDAY
1

SURROUND YOURSELF WITH PEOPLE
WHO INSPIRE YOU TO LIVE BOLDLY!

THURSDAY
2

Groundhog Day

NOTE TO SELF: YOU HAVE COME SO FAR!

FRIDAY
3

SATURDAY
4

YOU DON'T HAVE TO FIX EVERYTHING.

SUNDAY
5

DON'T FORGET:

FEBRUARY 2023

S	M	T	W	T	F	S
			1	2	3	4
5	6	7	8	9	10	11
12	13	14	15	16	17	18
19	20	21	22	23	24	25
26	27	28				

MARCH 2023

S	M	T	W	T	F	S
			1	2	3	4
5	6	7	8	9	10	11
12	13	14	15	16	17	18
19	20	21	22	23	24	25
26	27	28	29	30	31	

THIS WEEK'S HAPPY MOMENT:

MONDAY
6

Waitangi Day (NZ)

TUESDAY
7

TURN THE GRIND INTO A GRIN!

WEDNESDAY
8

THURSDAY
9

DO YOU HAVE ANY IDEA HOW STRONG YOU ARE?

FRIDAY
10

SATURDAY
11

IF YOU STUMBLE, MAKE IT PART OF THE DANCE.

SUNDAY
12

Abraham Lincoln's Birthday

DON'T FORGET:

FEBRUARY 2023

S	M	T	W	T	F	S
			1	2	3	4
5	6	7	8	9	10	11
12	13	14	15	16	17	18
19	20	21	22	23	24	25
26	27	28				

MARCH 2023

S	M	T	W	T	F	S
			1	2	3	4
5	6	7	8	9	10	11
12	13	14	15	16	17	18
19	20	21	22	23	24	25
26	27	28	29	30	31	

THIS WEEK'S HAPPY MOMENT:

MONDAY
13

THE GREATEST LOVE STORY: YOU + YOURSELF.

TUESDAY
14

Valentine's Day

WEDNESDAY
15

MAKE TODAY MATTER.

THURSDAY
16

WHAT'S YOUR THEME SONG? TURN THE VOLUME UP AND BELT IT OUT!

FRIDAY 17

SATURDAY 18

SUNDAY 19

KEEP SOME ROOM IN YOUR HEART FOR THE UNIMAGINABLE!

DON'T FORGET:

FEBRUARY 2023

S	M	T	W	T	F	S
			1	2	3	4
5	6	7	8	9	10	11
12	13	14	15	16	17	18
19	20	21	22	23	24	25
26	27	28				

MARCH 2023

S	M	T	W	T	F	S
			1	2	3	4
5	6	7	8	9	10	11
12	13	14	15	16	17	18
19	20	21	22	23	24	25
26	27	28	29	30	31	

THIS WEEK'S HAPPY MOMENT:

MONDAY
20

Presidents' Day

TUESDAY
21

DON'T FORGET TO CALL FOR BACKUP!
WE ALL NEED A LITTLE HELP SOMETIMES.

WEDNESDAY
22

Ash Wednesday (Lent begins)

THURSDAY
23

TREAT YOURSELF TO THAT FANCY
COFFEE. YOU DESERVE IT!

FRIDAY
24

BE THE MAGIC
MAKER. IT'S IN YOU.

SATURDAY
25

SUNDAY
26

DON'T FORGET:

THIS WEEK'S
HAPPY MOMENT:

FEBRUARY 2023

S	M	T	W	T	F	S
			1	2	3	4
5	6	7	8	9	10	11
12	13	14	15	16	17	18
19	20	21	22	23	24	25
26	27	28				

MARCH 2023

S	M	T	W	T	F	S
			1	2	3	4
5	6	7	8	9	10	11
12	13	14	15	16	17	18
19	20	21	22	23	24	25
26	27	28	29	30	31	

MONTHLY GOALS

NEW GOALS TO FOCUS ON

WHAT WORKED LAST MONTH

WHAT COULD BE BETTER

Where flowers
BLOOM
So does
HOPE

MARCH 2023

SUNDAY	MONDAY	TUESDAY	WEDNESDAY	THURSDAY	FRIDAY	SATURDAY
26	27	28	1	2	3	4
5	6 Purim begins	7	8 International Women's Day	9	10	11
12 Daylight Saving Time begins (USA, CAN)	13 Public Holiday (AUS: ACT, SA, TAS, VIC)	14	15	16	17 St. Patrick's Day	18
19 Mothering Sunday (UK)	20 Spring begins (Northern Hemisphere)	21	22 Ramadan begins	23	24	25
26	27	28	29	30	31	1

CREATURE OF HABIT

Track new goals or habits and watch your progress every month!

HABIT	1	2	3	4	5	6	7	8	9	10	11	12	13	14	15	16	17	18	19	20	21	22	23	24	25	26	27	28	29	30	31

MONDAY
27

PS: DON'T FORGET TO HAVE A GOOD TIME.

TUESDAY
28

WEDNESDAY
1

TREAT YOURSELF TO A DAY (OR EVEN JUST AN HOUR!) OF COMFORT.

THURSDAY
2

GIVE YOURSELF THE BENEFIT
OF THE DOUBT.

FRIDAY
3

SATURDAY
4

TAKE THE LEAP AND
TRY SOMETHING NEW!

SUNDAY
5

DON'T FORGET:

MARCH 2023

S	M	T	W	T	F	S
			1	2	3	4
5	6	7	8	9	10	11
12	13	14	15	16	17	18
19	20	21	22	23	24	25
26	27	28	29	30	31	

APRIL 2023

S	M	T	W	T	F	S
						1
2	3	4	5	6	7	8
9	10	11	12	13	14	15
16	17	18	19	20	21	22
23/30	24	25	26	27	28	29

THIS WEEK'S
HAPPY MOMENT:

2023 MARCH

MONDAY
6

Purim begins

TUESDAY
7

TRADE THE SELF-SABOTAGE FOR SOME SELF-CONFIDENCE.

WEDNESDAY
8

International Women's Day

THURSDAY
9

HAVE YOU TOLD YOUR LOVED ONES HOW MUCH YOU LOVE THEM?

FRIDAY
10

YOU'RE DOING
THIS BECAUSE
YOU WANT TO.

SATURDAY
11

SUNDAY
12

Daylight Saving Time begins (USA, CAN)

DON'T FORGET:

MARCH 2023

S	M	T	W	T	F	S
			1	2	3	4
5	6	7	8	9	10	11
12	13	14	15	16	17	18
19	20	21	22	23	24	25
26	27	28	29	30	31	

APRIL 2023

S	M	T	W	T	F	S
						1
2	3	4	5	6	7	8
9	10	11	12	13	14	15
16	17	18	19	20	21	22
23/30	24	25	26	27	28	29

THIS WEEK'S
HAPPY MOMENT:

2023 MARCH

MONDAY
13

LIVE LIFE. DON'T LET LIFE LIVE YOU.

Public Holiday (AUS: ACT, SA, TAS, VIC)

TUESDAY
14

WEDNESDAY
15

ALLOW YOURSELF TO GET LOST IN YOUR DAYDREAMS.

THURSDAY
16

YOU SHAMROCK THE WORLD!

FRIDAY
17

St. Patrick's Day

SATURDAY
18

SCATTER SEEDS
OF KINDNESS
WHEREVER YOU GO.

SUNDAY
19

Mothering Sunday (UK)

DON'T FORGET:

THIS WEEK'S
HAPPY MOMENT:

MARCH 2023

S	M	T	W	T	F	S
			1	2	3	4
5	6	7	8	9	10	11
12	13	14	15	16	17	18
19	20	21	22	23	24	25
26	27	28	29	30	31	

APRIL 2023

S	M	T	W	T	F	S
						1
2	3	4	5	6	7	8
9	10	11	12	13	14	15
16	17	18	19	20	21	22
23/30	24	25	26	27	28	29

2023 MARCH

MONDAY
20

Spring begins (Northern Hemisphere)

TUESDAY
21

HAPPINESS IS LIKE SPRING—IT ALWAYS BLOOMS AFTER THE DARKEST OF DAYS.

WEDNESDAY
22

Ramadan begins

THURSDAY
23

SOMETIMES TODAY'S PROBLEMS NEED TOMORROW TO SOLVE.

FRIDAY
24

WHY BE MOODY WHEN YOU CAN SHAKE YOUR BOOTY?

SATURDAY
25

SUNDAY
26

DON'T FORGET:

MARCH 2023

S	M	T	W	T	F	S
			1	2	3	4
5	6	7	8	9	10	11
12	13	14	15	16	17	18
19	20	21	22	23	24	25
26	27	28	29	30	31	

APRIL 2023

S	M	T	W	T	F	S
						1
2	3	4	5	6	7	8
9	10	11	12	13	14	15
16	17	18	19	20	21	22
23/30	24	25	26	27	28	29

THIS WEEK'S HAPPY MOMENT:

2023 MARCH/APRIL

MONDAY
27

DO SOMETHING NICE, EVEN IF IT'S NOT YOUR JOB.

TUESDAY
28

WEDNESDAY
29

FEARS ARE A CHANCE TO FLOURISH. HOW CAN YOU GROW?

THURSDAY
30

MADE IT TO FRIYAY!

FRIDAY
31

SATURDAY
1

April Fools' Day

IT'S NO JOKE HOW SPECTACULAR YOU ARE!

SUNDAY
2

Palm Sunday

DON'T FORGET:

MARCH 2023

S	M	T	W	T	F	S
			1	2	3	4
5	6	7	8	9	10	11
12	13	14	15	16	17	18
19	20	21	22	23	24	25
26	27	28	29	30	31	

APRIL 2023

S	M	T	W	T	F	S
						1
2	3	4	5	6	7	8
9	10	11	12	13	14	15
16	17	18	19	20	21	22
23/30	24	25	26	27	28	29

THIS WEEK'S HAPPY MOMENT:

MONTHLY GOALS

NEW GOALS TO FOCUS ON

WHAT WORKED LAST MONTH

WHAT COULD BE BETTER

ALLOW YOURSELF TO BE WHERE YOU ARE

APRIL 2023

SUNDAY	MONDAY	TUESDAY	WEDNESDAY	THURSDAY	FRIDAY	SATURDAY
26	27	28	29	30	31	1 April Fools' Day
2 Palm Sunday	3	4	5 Passover begins	6	7 Good Friday	8
9 Easter	10 Easter Monday (AUS, CAN, NZ, UK except SCT)	11	12	13	14	15
16	17	18 Tax Day	19	20	21 Eid al-Fitr begins	22 Earth Day
23/30	24	25 Anzac Day (AUS, NZ)	26	27	28 Workers' Memorial Day (UK)	29

CREATURE OF HABIT

Track new goals or habits and watch your progress every month!

HABIT	1	2	3	4	5	6	7	8	9	10	11	12	13	14	15	16	17	18	19	20	21	22	23	24	25	26	27	28	29	30	31

2023 **APRIL**

MONDAY
3

TUESDAY
4

HONORING YOUR NEEDS IS ONE OF THE GREATEST GIFTS YOU CAN GIVE YOURSELF.

WEDNESDAY
5

Passover begins

THURSDAY
6

LET YOURSELF BE A BEGINNER.

FRIDAY
7

Good Friday

WHAT IS GONE IS NOT AS GOOD AS WHAT IS COMING.

SATURDAY
8

SUNDAY
9

Easter

DON'T FORGET:

APRIL 2023

S	M	T	W	T	F	S
						1
2	3	4	5	6	7	8
9	10	11	12	13	14	15
16	17	18	19	20	21	22
23/30	24	25	26	27	28	29

MAY 2023

S	M	T	W	T	F	S
	1	2	3	4	5	6
7	8	9	10	11	12	13
14	15	16	17	18	19	20
21	22	23	24	25	26	27
28	29	30	31			

THIS WEEK'S HAPPY MOMENT:

2023 **APRIL**

MONDAY
10

LET YOUR POSITIVITY BRIGHTEN THE SKY!

Easter Monday (AUS, CAN, NZ, UK except SCT)

TUESDAY
11

WEDNESDAY
12

EVEN WHEN THE GOING GETS TOUGH, CHOOSE TO LOVE.

THURSDAY
13

TREAT YOURSELF LIKE A HOUSEPLANT: WITH PLENTY OF WATER AND LOTS OF SUN.

FRIDAY
14

SATURDAY
15

REMEMBER TO FORGIVE YOURSELF TOO.

SUNDAY
16

DON'T FORGET:

THIS WEEK'S HAPPY MOMENT:

APRIL 2023

S	M	T	W	T	F	S
						1
2	3	4	5	6	7	8
9	10	11	12	13	14	15
16	17	18	19	20	21	22
23/30	24	25	26	27	28	29

MAY 2023

S	M	T	W	T	F	S
	1	2	3	4	5	6
7	8	9	10	11	12	13
14	15	16	17	18	19	20
21	22	23	24	25	26	27
28	29	30	31			

2023 **APRIL**

MONDAY
17

TUESDAY
18

TOUGH TIMES NEVER LAST.

Tax Day

WEDNESDAY
19

THURSDAY
20

TODAY LOOKS LIKE A ***REALLY*** GOOD DAY.

FRIDAY
21

Eid al-Fitr begins

GO FIND YOUR RAINBOW AND SHINE ON!

SATURDAY
22

Earth Day

SUNDAY
23

DON'T FORGET:

APRIL 2023

S	M	T	W	T	F	S
						1
2	3	4	5	6	7	8
9	10	11	12	13	14	15
16	17	18	19	20	21	22
23/30	24	25	26	27	28	29

MAY 2023

S	M	T	W	T	F	S
	1	2	3	4	5	6
7	8	9	10	11	12	13
14	15	16	17	18	19	20
21	22	23	24	25	26	27
28	29	30	31			

THIS WEEK'S HAPPY MOMENT:

2023 **APRIL**

MONDAY
24

COFFEE IN ONE HAND,
CONFIDENCE IN THE OTHER.

TUESDAY
25

Anzac Day (AUS, NZ)

WEDNESDAY
26

YOU ARE INHERENTLY DESERVING
OF REST AND HAPPINESS.

THURSDAY
27

GLOW LIKE THE WHOLE UNIVERSE IS YOURS.

FRIDAY 28

Workers' Memorial Day (UK)

SATURDAY 29

SUNDAY 30

YOU'RE IN CONTROL OF WHATEVER YOU WANT TODAY TO BE.

DON'T FORGET:

APRIL 2023

S	M	T	W	T	F	S
						1
2	3	4	5	6	7	8
9	10	11	12	13	14	15
16	17	18	19	20	21	22
23/30	24	25	26	27	28	29

MAY 2023

S	M	T	W	T	F	S
	1	2	3	4	5	6
7	8	9	10	11	12	13
14	15	16	17	18	19	20
21	22	23	24	25	26	27
28	29	30	31			

THIS WEEK'S HAPPY MOMENT:

MONTHLY GOALS

NEW GOALS TO FOCUS ON

WHAT WORKED LAST MONTH

WHAT COULD BE BETTER

LIVE YOUR

Life LIKE

A COMPASS

NOT A *Clock*

MAY 2023

SUNDAY	MONDAY	TUESDAY	WEDNESDAY	THURSDAY	FRIDAY	SATURDAY
30	1	2	3	4	5 Cinco de Mayo	6
7	8	9	10	11	12	13
14 Mother's Day (USA, AUS, CAN, NZ)	15	16	17	18	19	20 Armed Forces Day
21	22 Victoria Day (CAN)	23	24	25 Shavuot begins	26	27
28	29 Memorial Day (USA); Spring Bank Holiday (UK)	30	31	1	2	3

CREATURE OF HABIT

Track new goals or habits and watch your progress every month!

HABIT	1	2	3	4	5	6	7	8	9	10	11	12	13	14	15	16	17	18	19	20	21	22	23	24	25	26	27	28	29	30	31

MONDAY
1

TUESDAY
2

CREATE A PLAYLIST WITH THE SONGS THAT MAKE YOU HAPPY, THEN DANCE!

WEDNESDAY
3

THURSDAY
4

LESS IS MORE. WHAT CAN YOU DO LESS OF?

FRIDAY
5

Cinco de Mayo

YOU'RE COOLER
THAN A CUCUMBER.

SATURDAY
6

SUNDAY
7

DON'T FORGET:

MAY 2023

S	M	T	W	T	F	S
	1	2	3	4	5	6
7	8	9	10	11	12	13
14	15	16	17	18	19	20
21	22	23	24	25	26	27
28	29	30	31			

JUNE 2023

S	M	T	W	T	F	S
				1	2	3
4	5	6	7	8	9	10
11	12	13	14	15	16	17
18	19	20	21	22	23	24
25	26	27	28	29	30	

THIS WEEK'S
HAPPY MOMENT:

2023 **MAY**

MONDAY
8

SAVOR THE MOMENT THAT YOU'RE IN RIGHT NOW.

TUESDAY
9

WEDNESDAY
10

GOOD MORNING. IT'S GOING TO BE A ***WONDERFUL*** DAY.

THURSDAY
11

BREATHE IN, BREATHE OUT. HOW DOES IT FEEL TO BE ALIVE TODAY?

FRIDAY 12

SATURDAY 13

SUNDAY 14

YOU'RE ONE OF A KIND!

Mother's Day (USA, AUS, CAN, NZ)

DON'T FORGET:

MAY 2023

S	M	T	W	T	F	S
	1	2	3	4	5	6
7	8	9	10	11	12	13
14	15	16	17	18	19	20
21	22	23	24	25	26	27
28	29	30	31			

JUNE 2023

S	M	T	W	T	F	S
				1	2	3
4	5	6	7	8	9	10
11	12	13	14	15	16	17
18	19	20	21	22	23	24
25	26	27	28	29	30	

THIS WEEK'S HAPPY MOMENT:

2023 **MAY**

MONDAY
15

TUESDAY
16

REAL GROWTH IS BEING MORE OF YOURSELF
AND LESS OF OTHERS' EXPECTATIONS.

WEDNESDAY
17

THURSDAY
18

THIS IS YOUR TAKE-A-BREAK COUPON. USE AS NEEDED!

FRIDAY
19

TODAY. IS. GOOD.

SATURDAY
20

Armed Forces Day

SUNDAY
21

DON'T FORGET:

MAY 2023

S	M	T	W	T	F	S
	1	2	3	4	5	6
7	8	9	10	11	12	13
14	15	16	17	18	19	20
21	22	23	24	25	26	27
28	29	30	31			

JUNE 2023

S	M	T	W	T	F	S
				1	2	3
4	5	6	7	8	9	10
11	12	13	14	15	16	17
18	19	20	21	22	23	24
25	26	27	28	29	30	

THIS WEEK'S HAPPY MOMENT:

MONDAY
22

BE A FLAMINGO IN A FLOCK OF PIGEONS.

Victoria Day (CAN)

TUESDAY
23

WEDNESDAY
24

NEVER FORGET HOW WILDLY CAPABLE YOU ARE.

THURSDAY
25

Shavuot begins

TAKE THE SCENIC ROUTE. EVERYONE NEEDS SOME BREATHING ROOM SOMETIMES.

FRIDAY 26

SATURDAY 27

TAKE TIME TO MAKE YOUR SOUL HAPPY.

SUNDAY 28

DON'T FORGET:

MAY 2023

S	M	T	W	T	F	S
	1	2	3	4	5	6
7	8	9	10	11	12	13
14	15	16	17	18	19	20
21	22	23	24	25	26	27
28	29	30	31			

JUNE 2023

S	M	T	W	T	F	S
				1	2	3
4	5	6	7	8	9	10
11	12	13	14	15	16	17
18	19	20	21	22	23	24
25	26	27	28	29	30	

THIS WEEK'S HAPPY MOMENT:

MONTHLY GOALS

NEW GOALS TO FOCUS ON

WHAT WORKED LAST MONTH

WHAT COULD BE BETTER

SEEK
TO FIND
THOSE
WHO ARE
KIND

JUNE 2023

SUNDAY	MONDAY	TUESDAY	WEDNESDAY	THURSDAY	FRIDAY	SATURDAY
28	29	30	31	1	2	3
4	5	6	7	8	9	10
11	12	13	14 Flag Day	15	16	17
18 Father's Day (USA, CAN, UK)	19 Juneteenth	20	21 Summer begins (Northern Hemisphere)	22	23	24
25	26	27	28 Eid al-Adha begins	29	30	1

CREATURE OF HABIT

Track new goals or habits and watch your progress every month!

HABIT	1	2	3	4	5	6	7	8	9	10	11	12	13	14	15	16	17	18	19	20	21	22	23	24	25	26	27	28	29	30	31

2023 MAY/JUNE

MONDAY
29

Memorial Day (USA); Spring Bank Holiday (UK)

TUESDAY
30

NEVER SELL YOURSELF SHORT.

WEDNESDAY
31

THURSDAY
1

GIVE YOURSELF THE OPPORTUNITY TO PROVE YOUR OWN INSECURITIES WRONG!

FRIDAY
2

LEADER OF THE
SELF-LOVE CLUB.

SATURDAY
3

SUNDAY
4

DON'T FORGET:

JUNE 2023

S	M	T	W	T	F	S
				1	2	3
4	5	6	7	8	9	10
11	12	13	14	15	16	17
18	19	20	21	22	23	24
25	26	27	28	29	30	

JULY 2023

S	M	T	W	T	F	S
						1
2	3	4	5	6	7	8
9	10	11	12	13	14	15
16	17	18	19	20	21	22
23/30	24/31	25	26	27	28	29

THIS WEEK'S
HAPPY MOMENT:

2023 JUNE

MONDAY
5

DON'T WORRY. CHOOSE HAPPY.

TUESDAY
6

WEDNESDAY
7

YOUR SMILE IS STUPENDOUS! SHOW IT OFF.

THURSDAY
8

YOU CAN'T POUR FROM AN EMPTY CUP. TAKE CARE OF YOURSELF.

FRIDAY
9

SATURDAY
10

UNPLUG TODAY! GO PLAY.

SUNDAY
11

DON'T FORGET:

JUNE 2023

S	M	T	W	T	F	S
				1	2	3
4	5	6	7	8	9	10
11	12	13	14	15	16	17
18	19	20	21	22	23	24
25	26	27	28	29	30	

JULY 2023

S	M	T	W	T	F	S
						1
2	3	4	5	6	7	8
9	10	11	12	13	14	15
16	17	18	19	20	21	22
23/30	24/31	25	26	27	28	29

THIS WEEK'S HAPPY MOMENT:

2023 JUNE

MONDAY
12

TUESDAY
13

REFUSE TO STRESS OVER THE THINGS YOU CANNOT CHANGE.

WEDNESDAY
14

Flag Day

THURSDAY
15

TAKE A DEEP BREATH AND JUMP IN. YOU'LL MAKE A SPLASH!

FRIDAY 16

SATURDAY 17

DEDICATE THIS WEEKEND TO REJUVENATION.

SUNDAY 18

Father's Day (USA, CAN, UK)

DON'T FORGET:

THIS WEEK'S HAPPY MOMENT:

JUNE 2023

S	M	T	W	T	F	S
				1	2	3
4	5	6	7	8	9	10
11	12	13	14	15	16	17
18	19	20	21	22	23	24
25	26	27	28	29	30	

JULY 2023

S	M	T	W	T	F	S
						1
2	3	4	5	6	7	8
9	10	11	12	13	14	15
16	17	18	19	20	21	22
23/30	24/31	25	26	27	28	29

MONDAY
19

IT'S OK TO SAY NO SOMETIMES.

Juneteenth

TUESDAY
20

WEDNESDAY
21

KEEP YOUR FACE TOWARD THE SUNSHINE!

Summer begins (Northern Hemisphere)

THURSDAY
22

JUST *TRY*. WHO KNOWS
WHAT COULD HAPPEN!

FRIDAY 23

SATURDAY 24

REMEMBER TO DRINK
SOME WATER!

SUNDAY 25

DON'T FORGET:

JUNE 2023

S	M	T	W	T	F	S
				1	2	3
4	5	6	7	8	9	10
11	12	13	14	15	16	17
18	19	20	21	22	23	24
25	26	27	28	29	30	

JULY 2023

S	M	T	W	T	F	S
						1
2	3	4	5	6	7	8
9	10	11	12	13	14	15
16	17	18	19	20	21	22
23/30	24/31	25	26	27	28	29

THIS WEEK'S
HAPPY MOMENT:

2023 JUNE/JULY

MONDAY
26

TUESDAY
27

ROOT YOURSELF IN THE LOVE THAT SURROUNDS YOU.

WEDNESDAY
28

Eid al-Adha begins

THURSDAY
29

HOW CAN YOU SPARK YOUR CREATIVITY TODAY?

FRIDAY
30

LIFE'S A PICNIC!

SATURDAY
1

Canada Day (CAN)

SUNDAY
2

DON'T FORGET:

THIS WEEK'S
HAPPY MOMENT:

JUNE 2023

S	M	T	W	T	F	S
				1	2	3
4	5	6	7	8	9	10
11	12	13	14	15	16	17
18	19	20	21	22	23	24
25	26	27	28	29	30	

JULY 2023

S	M	T	W	T	F	S
						1
2	3	4	5	6	7	8
9	10	11	12	13	14	15
16	17	18	19	20	21	22
23/30	24/31	25	26	27	28	29

MONTHLY GOALS

NEW GOALS TO FOCUS ON

WHAT WORKED LAST MONTH

WHAT COULD BE BETTER

THINGS WILL WORK OUT

JULY 2023

SUNDAY	MONDAY	TUESDAY	WEDNESDAY	THURSDAY	FRIDAY	SATURDAY
25	26	27	28	29	30	1 Canada Day (CAN)
2	3	4 Independence Day	5	6	7	8
9	10	11	12 Orangemen's Day—Battle of the Boyne (NIR)	13	14	15
16	17	18	19	20	21	22
23/30	24/31	25	26	27	28	29

CREATURE OF HABIT

Track new goals or habits and watch your progress every month!

HABIT	1	2	3	4	5	6	7	8	9	10	11	12	13	14	15	16	17	18	19	20	21	22	23	24	25	26	27	28	29	30	31

2023 **JULY**

MONDAY
3

YOU'RE AN ABSOLUTE FIRECRACKER!

TUESDAY
4

Independence Day

WEDNESDAY
5

R.E.S.P.E.C.T. YOURSELF.

THURSDAY
6

CULTIVATE YOUR CONFIDENCE AND WAVE IT PROUDLY!

FRIDAY 7

SATURDAY 8

CASH IN YOUR KARMA! YOU DESERVE SOMETHING NICE.

SUNDAY 9

DON'T FORGET:

JULY 2023

S	M	T	W	T	F	S
						1
2	3	4	5	6	7	8
9	10	11	12	13	14	15
16	17	18	19	20	21	22
23/30	24/31	25	26	27	28	29

AUGUST 2023

S	M	T	W	T	F	S
		1	2	3	4	5
6	7	8	9	10	11	12
13	14	15	16	17	18	19
20	21	22	23	24	25	26
27	28	29	30	31		

THIS WEEK'S HAPPY MOMENT:

MONDAY
10

TUESDAY
11

BE YOUR BIGGEST FAN! YOU'RE WORTH THE HYPE.

WEDNESDAY
12

Orangemen's Day—Battle of the Boyne (NIR)

THURSDAY
13

LEAN INTO THE SUNSHINE.

FRIDAY
14

WHAT SUMMER ACTIVITIES BRING YOU THE MOST JOY? DO ONE THIS WEEKEND!

SATURDAY
15

SUNDAY
16

DON'T FORGET:

JULY 2023

S	M	T	W	T	F	S
						1
2	3	4	5	6	7	8
9	10	11	12	13	14	15
16	17	18	19	20	21	22
23/30	24/31	25	26	27	28	29

AUGUST 2023

S	M	T	W	T	F	S
		1	2	3	4	5
6	7	8	9	10	11	12
13	14	15	16	17	18	19
20	21	22	23	24	25	26
27	28	29	30	31		

THIS WEEK'S HAPPY MOMENT:

2023 **JULY**

MONDAY
17

SOMETIMES STARTING OVER IS THE FIRST STEP FORWARD.

TUESDAY
18

WEDNESDAY
19

SET ASIDE AN HOUR TO DO
SOMETHING THAT BRINGS YOU PEACE.

THURSDAY
20

WHAT ADVENTURE WILL YOU GO ON THIS WEEKEND?

FRIDAY
21

SATURDAY
22

IF YOU'RE LOOKING FOR A SIGN, ***THIS IS IT.***

SUNDAY
23

DON'T FORGET:

JULY 2023

S	M	T	W	T	F	S
						1
2	3	4	5	6	7	8
9	10	11	12	13	14	15
16	17	18	19	20	21	22
23/30	24/31	25	26	27	28	29

AUGUST 2023

S	M	T	W	T	F	S
		1	2	3	4	5
6	7	8	9	10	11	12
13	14	15	16	17	18	19
20	21	22	23	24	25	26
27	28	29	30	31		

THIS WEEK'S HAPPY MOMENT:

2023 JULY

MONDAY
24

TUESDAY
25

KEEP LIFE ZESTY AND TRY SOMETHING NEW THIS WEEK!

WEDNESDAY
26

THURSDAY
27

YOU OWE YOURSELF THE LOVE YOU
SO EASILY GIVE TO OTHERS.

FRIDAY
28

BE THE LEADER OF THE POSITIVITY PARADE!

SATURDAY
29

SUNDAY
30

DON'T FORGET:

THIS WEEK'S HAPPY MOMENT:

JULY 2023

S	M	T	W	T	F	S
						1
2	3	4	5	6	7	8
9	10	11	12	13	14	15
16	17	18	19	20	21	22
23/30	24/31	25	26	27	28	29

AUGUST 2023

S	M	T	W	T	F	S
		1	2	3	4	5
6	7	8	9	10	11	12
13	14	15	16	17	18	19
20	21	22	23	24	25	26
27	28	29	30	31		

MONTHLY GOALS

NEW GOALS TO FOCUS ON

WHAT WORKED LAST MONTH

WHAT COULD BE BETTER

never REGRET ANYTHING that MADE you SMILE

AUGUST 2023

SUNDAY	MONDAY	TUESDAY	WEDNESDAY	THURSDAY	FRIDAY	SATURDAY
30	31	1	2	3	4	5
6	7 Summer Bank Holiday (SCT)	8	9	10	11	12
13	14	15	16	17	18	19
20	21	22	23	24	25	26
27	28 Summer Bank Holiday (UK except SCT)	29	30	31	1	2

CREATURE OF HABIT

Track new goals or habits and watch your progress every month!

HABIT	1	2	3	4	5	6	7	8	9	10	11	12	13	14	15	16	17	18	19	20	21	22	23	24	25	26	27	28	29	30	31

2023 JULY/AUGUST

MONDAY
31

JUST KEEP MOVING AND GROOVING.

TUESDAY
1

WEDNESDAY
2

YOU'RE THE MVP! MAKE EVERY DAY YOURS TO WIN.

THURSDAY
3

WONDERFUL THINGS OFTEN
ARRIVE WITHOUT NOTICE.

FRIDAY
4

SATURDAY
5

LEARNING HAS NO LIMITS.

SUNDAY
6

DON'T FORGET:

AUGUST 2023

S	M	T	W	T	F	S
		1	2	3	4	5
6	7	8	9	10	11	12
13	14	15	16	17	18	19
20	21	22	23	24	25	26
27	28	29	30	31		

SEPTEMBER 2023

S	M	T	W	T	F	S
					1	2
3	4	5	6	7	8	9
10	11	12	13	14	15	16
17	18	19	20	21	22	23
24	25	26	27	28	29	30

THIS WEEK'S
HAPPY MOMENT:

2023 **AUGUST**

MONDAY
7

Summer Bank Holiday (SCT)

TUESDAY
8

SOMETIMES A PERFECT TASK IS JUST A FINISHED ONE! CUT YOURSELF SOME SLACK.

WEDNESDAY
9

THURSDAY
10

HAPPINESS IS A HABIT.

FRIDAY
11

EMBRACE EVERYTHING
THAT MAKES YOU
WHO YOU ARE!

SATURDAY
12

SUNDAY
13

DON'T FORGET:

AUGUST 2023

S	M	T	W	T	F	S
		1	2	3	4	5
6	7	8	9	10	11	12
13	14	15	16	17	18	19
20	21	22	23	24	25	26
27	28	29	30	31		

SEPTEMBER 2023

S	M	T	W	T	F	S
					1	2
3	4	5	6	7	8	9
10	11	12	13	14	15	16
17	18	19	20	21	22	23
24	25	26	27	28	29	30

THIS WEEK'S
HAPPY MOMENT:

MONDAY
14

GIVE YOUR INNER CRITIC THE DAY OFF.

TUESDAY
15

WEDNESDAY
16

LET HAPPINESS BE YOUR COMPASS.

THURSDAY
17

BE MINDFUL EVEN IF YOUR MIND IS FULL.

FRIDAY 18

SATURDAY 19

SUNDAY 20

WHAT WAS YOUR HAPPY MOMENT THIS WEEK? NOW MAKE IT A HABIT!

DON'T FORGET:

AUGUST 2023

S	M	T	W	T	F	S
		1	2	3	4	5
6	7	8	9	10	11	12
13	14	15	16	17	18	19
20	21	22	23	24	25	26
27	28	29	30	31		

SEPTEMBER 2023

S	M	T	W	T	F	S
					1	2
3	4	5	6	7	8	9
10	11	12	13	14	15	16
17	18	19	20	21	22	23
24	25	26	27	28	29	30

THIS WEEK'S HAPPY MOMENT:

2023 **AUGUST**

MONDAY
21

TUESDAY
22

TRY SHUTTING EVERYTHING OFF FOR
AN HOUR (OR EVEN THE DAY)!

WEDNESDAY
23

THURSDAY
24

BE LOUD ABOUT THE THINGS
THAT ARE IMPORTANT TO YOU.

FRIDAY
25

GOALS HAVE NO
EXPIRATION DATE.

SATURDAY
26

SUNDAY
27

DON'T FORGET:

THIS WEEK'S
HAPPY MOMENT:

AUGUST 2023

S	M	T	W	T	F	S
		1	2	3	4	5
6	7	8	9	10	11	12
13	14	15	16	17	18	19
20	21	22	23	24	25	26
27	28	29	30	31		

SEPTEMBER 2023

S	M	T	W	T	F	S
					1	2
3	4	5	6	7	8	9
10	11	12	13	14	15	16
17	18	19	20	21	22	23
24	25	26	27	28	29	30

2023 AUGUST/SEPTEMBER

MONDAY
28

FOCUS ON WHAT IS WORKING.

Summer Bank Holiday (UK except SCT)

TUESDAY
29

WEDNESDAY
30

REMINDER: SELF-LOVE ISN'T SELFISH, IT'S IMPORTANT.

THURSDAY
31

GET OUT AND ENJOY THE LAST DAYS OF SUMMER!

FRIDAY
1

SATURDAY
2

SIMPLICITY IS BLISS.

SUNDAY
3

Father's Day (AUS, NZ)

DON'T FORGET:

AUGUST 2023

S	M	T	W	T	F	S
		1	2	3	4	5
6	7	8	9	10	11	12
13	14	15	16	17	18	19
20	21	22	23	24	25	26
27	28	29	30	31		

SEPTEMBER 2023

S	M	T	W	T	F	S
					1	2
3	4	5	6	7	8	9
10	11	12	13	14	15	16
17	18	19	20	21	22	23
24	25	26	27	28	29	30

THIS WEEK'S HAPPY MOMENT:

MONTHLY GOALS

NEW GOALS TO FOCUS ON

WHAT WORKED LAST MONTH

WHAT COULD BE BETTER

write YOUR own STORY

SEPTEMBER 2023

SUNDAY	MONDAY	TUESDAY	WEDNESDAY	THURSDAY	FRIDAY	SATURDAY
27	28	29	30	31	1	2
3 Father's Day (AUS, NZ)	4 Labor Day (USA, CAN)	5	6	7	8	9
10	11 Patriot Day	12	13	14	15 Rosh Hashanah begins	16
17	18	19	20	21	22	23 Autumn begins (Northern Hemisphere)
24 Yom Kippur begins	25	26	27	28	29 Sukkot begins	30

CREATURE OF HABIT

Track new goals or habits and watch your progress every month!

HABIT	1	2	3	4	5	6	7	8	9	10	11	12	13	14	15	16	17	18	19	20	21	22	23	24	25	26	27	28	29	30	31

MONDAY
4

Labor Day (USA, CAN)

TUESDAY
5

DO SOMETHING THAT YOUR FUTURE SELF WILL THANK YOU FOR.

WEDNESDAY
6

THURSDAY
7

GIVE YOURSELF A FEW EXTRA MINUTES TO STRETCH BEFORE BED TONIGHT!

FRIDAY
8

AFFIRMATION NATION!
YOU. ARE. GREAT.

SATURDAY
9

SUNDAY
10

DON'T FORGET:

THIS WEEK'S
HAPPY MOMENT:

SEPTEMBER 2023

S	M	T	W	T	F	S
					1	2
3	4	5	6	7	8	9
10	11	12	13	14	15	16
17	18	19	20	21	22	23
24	25	26	27	28	29	30

OCTOBER 2023

S	M	T	W	T	F	S
1	2	3	4	5	6	7
8	9	10	11	12	13	14
15	16	17	18	19	20	21
22	23	24	25	26	27	28
29	30	31				

2023 **SEPTEMBER**

MONDAY
11

HOW HAVE YOU SHOWN UP FOR YOURSELF LATELY?

Patriot Day

TUESDAY
12

WEDNESDAY
13

FOCUS ON ALL THAT YOU ARE
RATHER THAN ALL YOU ARE NOT.

THURSDAY
14

WORDS ARE POWERFUL. USE THEM
TOWARD YOURSELF AND OTHERS WISELY.

FRIDAY
15

Rosh Hashanah begins

SATURDAY
16

DO SMALL THINGS
WITH GREAT LOVE.

SUNDAY
17

DON'T FORGET:

THIS WEEK'S
HAPPY MOMENT:

SEPTEMBER 2023

S	M	T	W	T	F	S
					1	2
3	4	5	6	7	8	9
10	11	12	13	14	15	16
17	18	19	20	21	22	23
24	25	26	27	28	29	30

OCTOBER 2023

S	M	T	W	T	F	S
1	2	3	4	5	6	7
8	9	10	11	12	13	14
15	16	17	18	19	20	21
22	23	24	25	26	27	28
29	30	31				

2023 **SEPTEMBER**

MONDAY
18

TUESDAY
19

YOU ARE EXACTLY WHERE YOU NEED TO BE.

WEDNESDAY
20

THURSDAY
21

LIKE FRESH INK ON PAPER, WE NEED TIME TO REST BEFORE TURNING THE PAGE.

FRIDAY
22

LEAVES ARE FALLING AND AUTUMN IS CALLING! SAVOR IT.

SATURDAY
23

Autumn begins (Northern Hemisphere)

SUNDAY
24

Yom Kippur begins

DON'T FORGET:

SEPTEMBER 2023

S	M	T	W	T	F	S
					1	2
3	4	5	6	7	8	9
10	11	12	13	14	15	16
17	18	19	20	21	22	23
24	25	26	27	28	29	30

OCTOBER 2023

S	M	T	W	T	F	S
1	2	3	4	5	6	7
8	9	10	11	12	13	14
15	16	17	18	19	20	21
22	23	24	25	26	27	28
29	30	31				

THIS WEEK'S HAPPY MOMENT:

2023 **SEPTEMBER/OCTOBER**

MONDAY
25

EVERYTHING YOU'VE ACCOMPLISHED
SO FAR IS WORTH CELEBRATING.

TUESDAY
26

WEDNESDAY
27

PAT YOURSELF ON THE BACK FOR BEING SO AMAZING!

THURSDAY
28

LIFE IS BETTER IN PJ'S! RELAX!

FRIDAY 29

Sukkot begins

SATURDAY 30

PUT THE TO-DO LIST ON HOLD FOR TODAY. JUST BREATHE.

SUNDAY 1

DON'T FORGET:

SEPTEMBER 2023

S	M	T	W	T	F	S
					1	2
3	4	5	6	7	8	9
10	11	12	13	14	15	16
17	18	19	20	21	22	23
24	25	26	27	28	29	30

OCTOBER 2023

S	M	T	W	T	F	S
1	2	3	4	5	6	7
8	9	10	11	12	13	14
15	16	17	18	19	20	21
22	23	24	25	26	27	28
29	30	31				

THIS WEEK'S HAPPY MOMENT:

MONTHLY GOALS

NEW GOALS TO FOCUS ON

WHAT WORKED LAST MONTH

WHAT COULD BE BETTER

Dreaming,
AFTER ALL,
IS A FORM
OF
PLANNING

-Gloria Steinem

OCTOBER 2023

SUNDAY	MONDAY	TUESDAY	WEDNESDAY	THURSDAY	FRIDAY	SATURDAY
1	2	3	4	5	6	7
8	9 Columbus Day (USA); Indigenous Peoples' Day (USA); Thanksgiving Day (CAN)	10	11	12	13	14
15	16	17	18	19	20	21
22	23	24	25	26	27	28
29	30	31 Halloween	1	2	3	4

CREATURE OF HABIT

Track new goals or habits and watch your progress every month!

HABIT	1	2	3	4	5	6	7	8	9	10	11	12	13	14	15	16	17	18	19	20	21	22	23	24	25	26	27	28	29	30	31

2023 OCTOBER

MONDAY
2

TUESDAY
3

LET THE LOUDEST VOICE IN YOUR HEAD BE JOY!

WEDNESDAY
4

THURSDAY
5

YOUR ACCOMPLISHMENTS AND YOUR
FAILURES DO NOT DEFINE YOU.

FRIDAY
6

DON'T BE AFRAID TO LEAN ON THE PEOPLE YOU LOVE.

SATURDAY
7

SUNDAY
8

DON'T FORGET:

OCTOBER 2023

S	M	T	W	T	F	S
1	2	3	4	5	6	7
8	9	10	11	12	13	14
15	16	17	18	19	20	21
22	23	24	25	26	27	28
29	30	31				

NOVEMBER 2023

S	M	T	W	T	F	S
			1	2	3	4
5	6	7	8	9	10	11
12	13	14	15	16	17	18
19	20	21	22	23	24	25
26	27	28	29	30		

THIS WEEK'S HAPPY MOMENT:

2023 OCTOBER

MONDAY
9

GET A ONE-WAY TICKET FOR THE SELF-LOVE EXPRESS!

Columbus Day (USA); Indigenous Peoples' Day (USA); Thanksgiving Day (CAN)

TUESDAY
10

WEDNESDAY
11

GIVE THE GIFT OF TIME TO SOMEONE YOU CARE ABOUT. IT WILL MAKE YOU BOTH HAPPY!

THURSDAY
12

DON'T STOP UNTIL YOU'RE PROUD.

FRIDAY
13

SATURDAY
14

IT'S OK TO FEEL EVERYTHING YOU'RE FEELING.

SUNDAY
15

DON'T FORGET:

OCTOBER 2023

S	M	T	W	T	F	S
1	2	3	4	5	6	7
8	9	10	11	12	13	14
15	16	17	18	19	20	21
22	23	24	25	26	27	28
29	30	31				

NOVEMBER 2023

S	M	T	W	T	F	S
			1	2	3	4
5	6	7	8	9	10	11
12	13	14	15	16	17	18
19	20	21	22	23	24	25
26	27	28	29	30		

THIS WEEK'S HAPPY MOMENT:

2023 OCTOBER

MONDAY
16

TUESDAY
17

FIND BALANCE IN EVERYTHING.

WEDNESDAY
18

THURSDAY
19

HAS ANYONE EVER TOLD YOU YOU'RE A REAL GEM? BECAUSE YOU ARE.

FRIDAY
20

SATURDAY
21

SEEMS LIKE THE PERFECT DAY FOR A QUICK NAP. RELAX!

SUNDAY
22

DON'T FORGET:

THIS WEEK'S HAPPY MOMENT:

OCTOBER 2023

S	M	T	W	T	F	S
1	2	3	4	5	6	7
8	9	10	11	12	13	14
15	16	17	18	19	20	21
22	23	24	25	26	27	28
29	30	31				

NOVEMBER 2023

S	M	T	W	T	F	S
			1	2	3	4
5	6	7	8	9	10	11
12	13	14	15	16	17	18
19	20	21	22	23	24	25
26	27	28	29	30		

2023 **OCTOBER**

MONDAY
23

OWN YOUR MAGIC.

TUESDAY
24

WEDNESDAY
25

WELCOME TO LOUNGE TOWN! PJ'S AND COZINESS REQUIRED.

THURSDAY
26

HOW CAN YOU BE A POSITIVE FORCE FOR SOMEONE ELSE THIS WEEK?

FRIDAY
27

SATURDAY
28

YOU'RE THE ONE YOU'VE BEEN WAITING FOR!

SUNDAY
29

DON'T FORGET:

OCTOBER 2023

S	M	T	W	T	F	S
1	2	3	4	5	6	7
8	9	10	11	12	13	14
15	16	17	18	19	20	21
22	23	24	25	26	27	28
29	30	31				

NOVEMBER 2023

S	M	T	W	T	F	S
			1	2	3	4
5	6	7	8	9	10	11
12	13	14	15	16	17	18
19	20	21	22	23	24	25
26	27	28	29	30		

THIS WEEK'S HAPPY MOMENT:

MONTHLY GOALS

NEW GOALS TO FOCUS ON

WHAT WORKED LAST MONTH

WHAT COULD BE BETTER

BE gentle WITH yourself

NOVEMBER 2023

SUNDAY	MONDAY	TUESDAY	WEDNESDAY	THURSDAY	FRIDAY	SATURDAY
29	30	31	1	2	3	4
5 Daylight Saving Time ends (USA, CAN)	6	7 Election Day	8	9	10	11 Veterans Day (USA); Remembrance Day (CAN, UK)
12 Diwali begins	13	14	15	16	17	18
19	20	21	22	23 Thanksgiving Day	24	25
26	27	28	29	30 St. Andrew's Day (SCT)	1	2

CREATURE OF HABIT

Track new goals or habits and watch your progress every month!

HABIT	1	2	3	4	5	6	7	8	9	10	11	12	13	14	15	16	17	18	19	20	21	22	23	24	25	26	27	28	29	30	31

2023 OCTOBER/NOVEMBER

MONDAY
30

TUESDAY
31

NOTHING TURNS A BAD MOOD INTO A GOOD ONE LIKE CHOCOLATE.

Halloween

WEDNESDAY
1

THURSDAY
2

BE PATIENT WITH YOURSELF. WE ALL NEED A LITTLE COMPASSION.

FRIDAY
3

SATURDAY
4

GET THOSE ENDORPHINS! MOVE YOUR BODY IN A WAY THAT FEELS GOOD.

SUNDAY
5

Daylight Saving Time ends (USA, CAN)

DON'T FORGET:

NOVEMBER 2023

S	M	T	W	T	F	S
			1	2	3	4
5	6	7	8	9	10	11
12	13	14	15	16	17	18
19	20	21	22	23	24	25
26	27	28	29	30		

DECEMBER 2023

S	M	T	W	T	F	S
					1	2
3	4	5	6	7	8	9
10	11	12	13	14	15	16
17	18	19	20	21	22	23
24/31	25	26	27	28	29	30

THIS WEEK'S HAPPY MOMENT:

2023 **NOVEMBER**

MONDAY
6

YOU DESERVE SOME EXTRA Z'S!

TUESDAY
7

Election Day

WEDNESDAY
8

YOU CAN DO WHATEVER YOU WANT!

THURSDAY
9

STOP LETTING WHO YOU WERE TALK
YOU OUT OF WHO YOU'RE BECOMING.

FRIDAY 10

SATURDAY 11

Veterans Day (USA); Remembrance Day (CAN, UK)

SUNDAY 12

START YOUR DAY
WITH A DANCE PARTY
AND GROOVE!

Diwali begins

DON'T FORGET:

NOVEMBER 2023

S	M	T	W	T	F	S
			1	2	3	4
5	6	7	8	9	10	11
12	13	14	15	16	17	18
19	20	21	22	23	24	25
26	27	28	29	30		

DECEMBER 2023

S	M	T	W	T	F	S
					1	2
3	4	5	6	7	8	9
10	11	12	13	14	15	16
17	18	19	20	21	22	23
24/31	25	26	27	28	29	30

THIS WEEK'S
HAPPY MOMENT:

2023 **NOVEMBER**

MONDAY
13

TUESDAY
14

WHAT ARE YOU GRATEFUL FOR? DON'T FORGET TO INCLUDE YOURSELF!

WEDNESDAY
15

THURSDAY
16

LIKE FLECKS OF GOLD, EVERY NEW EXPERIENCE MAKES YOU RICHER.

FRIDAY
17

TODAY'S SELF-CARE MENU: H2O, SWEATPANTS, CHOCOLATE.

SATURDAY
18

SUNDAY
19

DON'T FORGET:

NOVEMBER 2023

S	M	T	W	T	F	S
			1	2	3	4
5	6	7	8	9	10	11
12	13	14	15	16	17	18
19	20	21	22	23	24	25
26	27	28	29	30		

DECEMBER 2023

S	M	T	W	T	F	S
					1	2
3	4	5	6	7	8	9
10	11	12	13	14	15	16
17	18	19	20	21	22	23
24/31	25	26	27	28	29	30

THIS WEEK'S HAPPY MOMENT:

2023 NOVEMBER

MONDAY
20

TAKE A MOMENT TO MARVEL AT THE MIRACLE THAT IS *YOU*.

TUESDAY
21

WEDNESDAY
22

GIVE YOURSELF THE FREEDOM TO INDULGE!

THURSDAY
23

Thanksgiving Day

YOUR PRESENCE MATTERS, EVEN
IN THE MOST SUBTLE WAYS.

FRIDAY
24

SATURDAY
25

REMEMBER TO
HAVE FUN TODAY!

SUNDAY
26

DON'T FORGET:

THIS WEEK'S
HAPPY MOMENT:

NOVEMBER 2023

S	M	T	W	T	F	S
			1	2	3	4
5	6	7	8	9	10	11
12	13	14	15	16	17	18
19	20	21	22	23	24	25
26	27	28	29	30		

DECEMBER 2023

S	M	T	W	T	F	S
					1	2
3	4	5	6	7	8	9
10	11	12	13	14	15	16
17	18	19	20	21	22	23
24/31	25	26	27	28	29	30

2023 NOVEMBER/DECEMBER

MONDAY
27

TUESDAY
28

BE YOU, NOT THEM.

WEDNESDAY
29

THURSDAY
30

DWELL ON WHAT'S POSSIBLE.

St. Andrew's Day (SCT)

FRIDAY
1

DO MORE OF WHAT
MAKES YOU HAPPY.

SATURDAY
2

SUNDAY
3

DON'T FORGET:

THIS WEEK'S
HAPPY MOMENT:

NOVEMBER 2023

S	M	T	W	T	F	S
			1	2	3	4
5	6	7	8	9	10	11
12	13	14	15	16	17	18
19	20	21	22	23	24	25
26	27	28	29	30		

DECEMBER 2023

S	M	T	W	T	F	S
					1	2
3	4	5	6	7	8	9
10	11	12	13	14	15	16
17	18	19	20	21	22	23
24/31	25	26	27	28	29	30

MONTHLY GOALS

NEW GOALS TO FOCUS ON

WHAT WORKED LAST MONTH

WHAT COULD BE BETTER

EVERY ending IS A NEW Beginning

DECEMBER 2023

SUNDAY	MONDAY	TUESDAY	WEDNESDAY	THURSDAY	FRIDAY	SATURDAY
26	27	28	29	30	1	2
3	4	5	6	7 Hanukkah begins; Pearl Harbor Day	8	9
10	11	12	13	14	15	16
17	18	19	20	21 Winter begins (Northern Hemisphere)	22	23
24/31 Christmas Eve (24th) New Year's Eve (31st)	25 Christmas Day	26 Kwanzaa begins; Boxing Day (AUS, CAN, NZ, UK)	27	28	29	30

CREATURE OF HABIT

Track new goals or habits and watch your progress every month!

HABIT	1	2	3	4	5	6	7	8	9	10	11	12	13	14	15	16	17	18	19	20	21	22	23	24	25	26	27	28	29	30	31

2023 **DECEMBER**

MONDAY
4

BE YOURSELF. YOU NEVER KNOW WHO YOU'RE INSPIRING.

TUESDAY
5

WEDNESDAY
6

EVERYONE HAS TO START SOMEWHERE. SO BEGIN!

THURSDAY
7

Hanukkah begins; Pearl Harbor Day

SPREAD SOME CHEER AND LIGHT UP SOMEONE'S DAY!

FRIDAY
8

SATURDAY
9

EMBRACE YOUR JOURNEY.

SUNDAY
10

DON'T FORGET:

DECEMBER 2023

S	M	T	W	T	F	S
					1	2
3	4	5	6	7	8	9
10	11	12	13	14	15	16
17	18	19	20	21	22	23
24/31	25	26	27	28	29	30

JANUARY 2024

S	M	T	W	T	F	S
	1	2	3	4	5	6
7	8	9	10	11	12	13
14	15	16	17	18	19	20
21	22	23	24	25	26	27
28	29	30	31			

THIS WEEK'S HAPPY MOMENT:

2023 DECEMBER

MONDAY
11

TUESDAY
12

CHASE ALL YOUR DREAMS. YOU'LL CATCH MORE THAN YOU THINK!

WEDNESDAY
13

THURSDAY
14

SELF-LOVE IS A SUPERPOWER.

FRIDAY
15

THERE'S *SNOW* PLACE LIKE HOME.

SATURDAY
16

SUNDAY
17

DON'T FORGET:

THIS WEEK'S HAPPY MOMENT:

DECEMBER 2023

S	M	T	W	T	F	S
					1	2
3	4	5	6	7	8	9
10	11	12	13	14	15	16
17	18	19	20	21	22	23
24/31	25	26	27	28	29	30

JANUARY 2024

S	M	T	W	T	F	S
	1	2	3	4	5	6
7	8	9	10	11	12	13
14	15	16	17	18	19	20
21	22	23	24	25	26	27
28	29	30	31			

2023 DECEMBER

MONDAY
18

REFLECT ON ALL THAT YOU HAVE ACCOMPLISHED!

TUESDAY
19

WEDNESDAY
20

OH, LOOK! IT'S COMFORT O'CLOCK!

THURSDAY
21

Winter begins (Northern Hemisphere)

YOU *ARE* A SUCCESS, EVEN IF YOU DON'T ALWAYS FEEL LIKE IT!

FRIDAY 22

SATURDAY 23

YOU'RE A RAY OF SUNSHINE.

SUNDAY 24

Christmas Eve

DON'T FORGET:

DECEMBER 2023

S	M	T	W	T	F	S
					1	2
3	4	5	6	7	8	9
10	11	12	13	14	15	16
17	18	19	20	21	22	23
24/31	25	26	27	28	29	30

JANUARY 2024

S	M	T	W	T	F	S
	1	2	3	4	5	6
7	8	9	10	11	12	13
14	15	16	17	18	19	20
21	22	23	24	25	26	27
28	29	30	31			

THIS WEEK'S HAPPY MOMENT:

2023 DECEMBER

MONDAY
25

Christmas Day

TUESDAY
26

EXIST POWERFULLY.

Kwanzaa begins; Boxing Day (AUS, CAN, NZ, UK)

WEDNESDAY
27

THURSDAY
28

HOW **BEAUTIFULLY** YOU'VE GROWN SINCE LAST YEAR!

FRIDAY
29

SATURDAY
30

SO MUCH IS POSSIBLE! WHAT ARE YOU LOOKING FORWARD TO IN 2024?

SUNDAY
31

New Year's Eve

DON'T FORGET:

THIS WEEK'S HAPPY MOMENT:

DECEMBER 2023

S	M	T	W	T	F	S
					1	2
3	4	5	6	7	8	9
10	11	12	13	14	15	16
17	18	19	20	21	22	23
24/31	25	26	27	28	29	30

JANUARY 2024

S	M	T	W	T	F	S
	1	2	3	4	5	6
7	8	9	10	11	12	13
14	15	16	17	18	19	20
21	22	23	24	25	26	27
28	29	30	31			

NOTES AND INSPIRATION

NOTES AND INSPIRATION

Jewish and Muslim holidays begin at sundown.

Published by Sourcebooks
P.O. Box 4410, Naperville, Illinois 60567-4410
(630) 961-3900
sourcebooks.com

Printed and bound in China.
OGP 10 9 8 7 6 5 4 3 2 1

APPOINTMENT

APPOINTMENT

APPOINTMENT

APPOINTMENT

APPOINTMENT

APPOINTMENT

APPOINTMENT

APPOINTMENT

APPOINTMENT

APPOINTMENT

APPOINTMENT

APPOINTMENT

MEETING

MEETING

MEETING

MEETING

MEETING

MEETING

MEETING

MEETING

MEETING

MEETING

MEETING

BIRTHDAY!

BIRTHDAY!

BIRTHDAY!

BIRTHDAY!

BIRTHDAY!

Stay Strong BE Positive

Explore MORE

YOU ARE ENOUGH

NOTE TO SELF

NOTE TO SELF

NOTE TO SELF

NOTE TO SELF

NOTE TO SELF

NOTE TO SELF

NOTE TO SELF

NOTE TO SELF

NOTE TO SELF

NOTE TO SELF

NOTE TO SELF

CELEBRATE!

CELEBRATE!

CELEBRATE!

CELEBRATE!

CELEBRATE!

CELEBRATE!

CELEBRATE!

CELEBRATE!

CELEBRATE!

CELEBRATE!

CELEBRATE!

CELEBRATE!

PLANS

PLANS

PLANS

PLANS

PLANS

PLANS

PLANS

PLANS

PLANS

PLANS

PLANS

BIRTHDAY!

BIRTHDAY!

BIRTHDAY!

BIRTHDAY!

BIRTHDAY!

BIRTHDAY!

GOOD VIBES

DAY OFF

DAY OFF

DAY OFF

DAY OFF

DAY OFF

DAY OFF

DAY OFF

DAY OFF

DAY OFF

DAY OFF

DUE DATE!

DUE DATE!

DUE DATE!

DUE DATE!

DUE DATE!

DUE DATE!

DUE DATE!

DUE DATE!

DUE DATE!

DUE DATE!

DUE DATE!

DUE DATE!

HOORAY!
HOORAY!
HOORAY!
HOORAY!
HOORAY!
HOORAY!
SELF CARE
SELF CARE
SELF CARE
SELF CARE
SELF CARE
SELF CARE
SELF CARE
SELF CARE
SELF CARE
SELF CARE
SELF CARE
PACK your THINGS
get LOST
TRAVEL
PACK your THINGS
DREAM IT. PLAN IT. DO IT.
TRAVEL
PACK your THINGS
get LOST
TRAVEL
REFRESH
REFRESH
REFRESH
Make TODAY GREAT
TREAT YO' SELF!
TREAT YO' SELF!